JACK MAPANJE

SKIPPING
WITHOUT ROPES

BLOODAXE BOOKS

ISBN: 1 85224 412 7

First published 1998 by
Bloodaxe Books Ltd,
P.O. Box 1SN,
Newcastle upon Tyne NE99 1SN.

Bloodaxe Books Ltd acknowledges
the financial assistance of Northern Arts.

Cover printing by J. Thomson Colour Printers Ltd, Glasgow.

Printed in Great Britain by
Cromwell Press Ltd, Trowbridge, Wiltshire.

Acknowledgements

Acknowledgements are due to the editors of the following publications where some of these poems first appeared: *Illuminations, Index on Censorship, London Magazine, Poetry Scotland, Poetry Wales, Scotland on Sunday, Stand, Upstart!* and *Wasafiri.*

I am indebted to Ludo Pieters Guest Writer's Fund, part of the larger Prince Barnhard Fund, The Netherlands, and Martin Mooij and his staff at Rotterdam Poetry International; the Authors' Foundation and the Kathleen Blundell Trust, Southern Arts Board and the Royal Literary Fund for their welcome financial support at the most critical stages of the development of the original manuscript of this selection.

Many thanks to Martin Banham and colleagues in the School of English, University of Leeds; Stephen Ellis and staff at African Studies Centre, University of Leiden; Dennis Walder and Valerie Bishop at the Open University, Milton Keynes, and the Nivens who gave me free access to their lovely attic in Eden House, Milton Keynes, from where this collection was finally restructured.

(Leiden, The Netherlands & York, England, 1998)

Contents

Dedication

(for Mercy, Judith, Lunda, Likambale, friends)

I thought I would offer you more muscular
Lines to help you reach the summits of this
Wandering seclusion without the tether; I

Remember pledging to myself I would plot
My own hope for you to surf these swells
Forever lashing our shores, a pledge I feared

I would never deliver but *pole sana** and may
These narrative symbols ease the torrents of
Your haven instead, may you skip your globe

More defiantly without my leash, with your
Hope recovered, may the bedrock of chuckle
Treasured heal our blisters with tons of love!

* Kiswahili for 'I am sorry, many apologies, etc'.

1 *From Mikuyu Prison to Exile*

The Following Dawn the Boots

The following dawn
I woke up to the reality of prison
boots, jangling keys and streaks of the golden sun
my bones, muscles and joints –
my whole new plight stiff

'The most dangerous rebels start out here
they may then be moved to other minor prisons
or perhaps promoted to the general cells inside
even that legendary gang of four came here first
at dusk, after lock-up, I commanded my guards
to chain them to the stocks in the cell you slept last night
(you have never heard notables
crying like naughty children!)
the next day the rebels were released
although the Special Branch who liberated them
refused to inscribe their names and signatures
in Mikuyu Prison Gate Books
as they had done when they brought in the prisoners
that's when we saw something suspicious
about their kind of liberation
so when we heard radio announcements
about their intention to cross the border at Mwanza
and their supposed accident there
the guards on duty hastened to bear witness
to the Mikuyu Gate Book inscriptions
of the Special Branch who had freed their eminence –
but, truly, men have been reprieved within days here
welcome home.'

The guard commander had intended
the tale to chill me into submission
from the first day of my arrival
he wanted no hunger strikes
no jumping over prison fences
no protests, no nonsense in his prison
he invoked my university mentors
the country's most 'notorious' rebels

demagogues and others who had felt
the grip and blister of his Sheffield
handcuffs, leg-irons, chains without blinking;
I embraced only his tale of the Gate Book engravings
imagining someone found it mattered some day.

Skipping Without Rope

I will, I will skip without your rope
Since you say I should not, I cannot
Borrow your son's skipping rope to
Exercise my limbs, I will skip without

Your rope as you say even the lace
I want will hang my neck until I die
I will create my own rope, my own
Hope and skip without your rope as

You insist I do not require to stretch
My limbs fixed by these fevers of your
Reeking sweat and your prison walls
I will, will skip with my forged hope;

Watch, watch me skip without your
Rope watch me skip with my hope
A-one, a-two, a-three, a-four, a-five
I will, a-seven, I do, will skip, a-ten,

Eleven, I will skip without, will skip
Within and skip I do without your
Rope but with my hope; and I will,
Will always skip you dull, will skip

Your silly rules, skip your filthy walls
Your weevil pigeon peas, skip your
Scorpions, skip your Excellency Life
Glory; I do, you don't, I can, you can't,

I will, you won't, I see, you don't, I
Sweat, you don't, I will, will wipe my
Gluey brow then wipe you at a stroke
I will, will wipe your horrid, stinking,

Vulgar prison rules, will wipe you all
Then hop about, hop about my cell, my
Home, the mountains, my globe as your
Sparrow hops about your prison yard

Without your hope, without your rope
I swear, I will skip without your rope, I
Declare, I will have you take me to your
Showers to bathe me where I can resist

This singing child you want to shape me
I'll fight your rope, your rules, your hope
As your sparrow does under your super-
vision! Guards! Take us for the shower!

Our Doctor Mr Ligomeka

(in memoriam)

I do not know why you return today
shouting at Mikuyu Prison guards that
you wish to detect the effect of *fansidar* your
WHO brand of malaria tablets on your patients,
'Open the gates for Mapanje!'
when the timid prison guards bring
me to your Sick Bay you demand privacy
'So I can have a proper look at his abscess!'
and as they reluctantly retire we have a soft laugh –
how nervously the idiots accept doctors' orders!

But you have come to tell me the story of my death,
you clarify, 'The nurses at the General are grieving
your death which some authority has devised,
I came to verify for myself, now that I know, I
will march you to the full view of the General!'
How you plan to perform this feat bemuses
but the message is clear,
when another bout of chronic malaria strikes
I must not be excited about
the new brands of quinine the prison offers
they could be poisons

Besides Martin Kanyuka, student, colleague, brother
has just been accidentalised,
'What I detest most is why they refused to let
me do the post-mortem when they said it was
just another accident!'
When you name three other university friends
disappeared in my short absence
my voice falters fearing,
'Won't you too vanish if they discover
the tricks you perform for us in prison?'

My dear doctor, you came to serve us
after inveterate wars for our medical liberation,
our appeals had flown to the freedom lovers
of the globe through friends, dedicated strangers
and official bags before you were offered to us,
the weeping blisters and thick boils you exploded
on our groins and between our buttocks
could not have been for nothing
how could we have dreamt them up
with buttocks already inured beyond baboons?

Do you recall the bones that clinked
squatting before you and the eyes
deep in drooping sockets pleading
for your prescription of valiums
to manage Mikuyu's sleepless nights?
And that smelly lump of *nsima* you
extracted from CheJumo's ears was
no mean madness, CheJumo frankly
sought to protect his ears from the tyrant's
tedious tales that had damned him here!
could he have invented delirium
for cheek, cheer, valiums?

So when we heard you too have been
disappeared today we are not surprised
but pray that wherever you are you might
still shelter the patients of the Sick Bay
of this prison you have left behind.

Season's Greetings for Celia (BC)

They say when God closes one door
He opens a window to let in the sun

Celia, your season's greetings arrived
In time of despair, after I had signed

My life out by signing the Detention
Order insisted upon by Life President

Who wishes us to rot, rot, rot forever
In this prison but your white and red

Roses invoke that War of the Roses I
Battled to comprehend to achieve my

A-levels, the green English landscape
Summons the Romantics I explored

Under the billowing smoke of paraffin
Tin-can lamps once upon the tough terrain

I thought I had left behind and how did
You hope to be remembered when you

Mark your name merely as Celia (BC)?
If the parentheticals are the British Council,

10 Spring Gardens, London, I recall no one
By that name there, my British Council

Programme organiser with whom I shared
My *London Magazine* poems was called

Sheila, I think, and why, why of all those
Bags and bags of protest mail which harass

The Post Office Sorting Centre everyday
As oblique couriers convey, why did only

Your postcard from London and another
From The Hague choose to slip past our

Strict mail sorters at this crucial moment,
What bribe did you provide the Officer-in-

Charge of prison for him to chance me to
His office to peruse your mail from over-

seas, defying the edict from the life-despot
And risking his life and mine? No matter

Your season's greetings Celia have thawed
Our anguish furnishing these rancid prison

Walls with much sought after night jasmine;
Now the cliché glowers: somewhere some-

one we do not know cares – and that dear
Celia is all the prisoner needs to know!

Hector's Slapping of Mama's Brother

I

Amnesty came like a whirlwind gathering
The courtyard's brown leaves, bird feathers,
Blanket threads, dust, tossing them about,
Twirling them through arid water drainages
To the world outside, Hector and the others
Were gone! Today with the marabous un-
caged, leaving the present aching oversights
And chasms for the black-wing stilts to wade
Through the swamps of the vast marshland
They have left behind and to scour this frog
Roe as the mosquitoes wail on their lily basins
Around the wash, now that Hector and more
Than twenty marabous have been liberated
Leaving us alone, unwanted, sterile, I dread
The time our turn will come, shall we sing
Those praises to God throughout the night as
The marabous temporarily held in the New
Building Wing of the prison did before being
Let loose, shall we smile at one another freed
After those wars we have endured over food,
Medicines, freedom, gods, these many years?

II

Hector's last battle over my valiums was bitter
'I have no more valiums left,' I try to explain
'Use your influence then!' Hector barks back;
I run into my cell to cry the hurt to sleep, when
I hear Hector's war with another mate erupting
Mainly frustrated by my valiums, the guards
Assault the courtyard truncheoned for murder
Only to detach the bleeding adversaries then
Lock them up in punishment cells chained to
The stocks, handcuffed, leg-ironed and naked
No water, no food, three buckets of cold water
Poured onto their frigid bodies, then felled on
The cold cement floor to swim for three days;

Today, I still hear Hector's comrade in his cell
Shrieking, remembering his mother. The war
Had begun with Hector boasting only he was
The man in Mikuyu for plucking the temper
To bruise life-despot's concubine's brother in
A brawl; Hector had claimed Mama's brother
Had breached their New Bakery's overtime
Intruding into their shifts and insisting on their
Adulation of his management of the bakery
The 'royal family' had snaffled; he had argued
His comrade had only drunk himself to shit!

III

Today those marabous are gone, actually set free,
Leaving us to recall the order the cell suffered to
Dossier Hector's battle for the Officer-in-Charge or
Else; I hear one proposition from the corner cockle,
'We must swear the war was over breadcrumbs
Which inmates on Special Diet had offered both
Combatants, their scramble for breadcrumbs has
Turned this nasty – that way OC will comprehend
Why we all need Special Diet!' Peals of laughter;
Another proposal ensues: let's offer the fighters'
Tribal colours as cause thus nettling life-despot's
Dictate on contact and dialogue already crumbling
'No!' issues from the corner, 'Let's tell the truth:
Marabou Hector was being frog-puffy to presume
Only he could have staked the slapping of Mama's
Loathed brother, nobody could stand the boast.' I
Remember us finally resolving that the battle was
Not to be about my valiums lest the OC banned
Those too; that night I recall sitting on my empty
Toilet, picking a pencil lead piece from my kinked
Hair, scratching my toilet paper for *more valiums*!

When Release Began Like a Biblical Parable

When the prison gates opened for apostle Simon
Peter who was sleeping, chained-double, guarded
By four squads of four Roman soldiers each; when
The angel's blinding flash tapped his quiescent side
The decisive chains on his blistered wrists suddenly
Dropping, when he belted up, the soundless sandals
Springing as he gathered his cloak around him on his
Way out, why, why did Peter not believe the vision
Until the last solid bar gave way on the Lord's own
Terms, the angel abandoning him unfettered outside,
Alone, as The Rock, liberated from Herod's clutches
Returned to his praying Antioch Church, stunned?

And why should this firefly at the back of another Land
Rover whose bleached canvas stutters in the whining
Wind speeding nowhere believe; why must I believe
Minded by these nervous guards as my Special Branch
Driver ravages his boiled groundnuts without a wink;
Why should my crumb of lifebuoy, my toothbrush with-
out its teeth, my toothpaste flattened clean, this partner
Of holed Levi's shoes, this polythene kilo of sugar (for
Porridge wherever I am going said Officer-in-Charge)
Can this be the reprieve of this flustered Peter, the clod,
Your late disciple, Lord, without the staff to lean on?
Let the dazzling dust of distant familiar mountains,

Let these eternally dry maize fields, the truncated leaf-
less mango trees that feel taller than bluegums (Your
'Ephpheta', Lord, brings such clash of memories I did
Not dream I would ever see again!), let peculiar colours
Soak up then, let the Land Rover's rails rattle as I blink
At my Officer-in-Charge, 'We do not know what it is,
As you know, nobody tells us anything but if it's transfer
To another prison, take your sugar, if further questioning
Further charges, we'll welcome you back, if release, best
Wishes, remember the friends you leave behind, other-
wise, we'll note the Gate Book names of your assailants
For your wife and children or for posterity, good luck!

Our Friend Police Inspector General

I

Forty-three months ago he frolicked as
Chief of Special Branch, boasting infinite
Access to the ubiquitous face on the walls
Of the country's wards; 'I report directly
To him!' he pointed at the despot's image
On his office wall; forty-three months today
He gloated over being Catholic too though
Slipped; could fellow Catholics trust each
Other then with the truth nothing but what
Might have riled the Life President to direct
His officers to arrest and detain? 'Tell me
Who reported you directly to HE, you have
The full protection of my force, I myself
Will implore the Life President's clemency!'
When I offered my forehead wrinkles for
His repentance, he taunted me with,'You
Must pray three Hail Marys of your Rosary
For his Eminence to forgive and to review
Your Friday 25 September, 1987, detention.'

II

But today after his three Hail Marys have
Become my stinking three and half years
And his promotion to Inspector General
Of the country's police, we have met again
He anxious to please, me suspicious about
This brusque invitation to his catholic office –
His antique scroll of stubborn tales unlocks:
He has been trying to change the monster's
Spots since we last spoke, 'Glance at this
January memo to HE,' he retorts, 'What
Does the margin of my memo to him say?'
I see five names with 'Approved' in black
Ink against the first four, 'Never' against
The fifth, mine, inscribed by His Excellency's
Initials which he always dated. 'My friend,
You were prisoner *never* to be freed in those
January and February releases you missed.

III

'But today, I flashed another card, Presidents
In other countries free political prisoners on
Their official birthdays, on HE's next week,
Why doesn't HE in his wisdom reconsider
Our story of those political prisoners who in
Our view have repented and will be under
Your Excellency's trusted police surveillance
Anyway, though I hate to bring this list of only
One political prisoner, your Excellency, Sir?'
He fishes out his latest memo to HE for my
Tears to bear my name capped in the middle
Of his memo. 'Do you see what's on the margin
Of my May memo to His Excellency?' When
I read 'Approved', see Life President's dated
Initials, my heart sinks, my eyes boggle as he
Points at HE's portrait on the wall and declares,
'HE is pleased to have you released, return to
Your wife and children before HE reshuffles
His cards, at this point only three people know
You are being released, HE, myself, yourself!'
As his words begin to mean my unshackled
Feet linger pondering 10 May 1991 outside!

Tamya's Shepherd's Pie
(10 May 1991)

Child, this shepherd's pie you offer this starved
stomach this late Friday afternoon, this china and

stainless knife and fork you place in his hand, this
glass of orange, your civil genuflection, your voice

so delicate and your wonder at the return of another
denuded memory witnessing the purple jacarandas

strewn on the rocks and avenues of Zomba plateau;
my dear child, do not ask where this bundle of blunt

tissue before you comes from nor where it proceeds;
having left behind other unsullied souls fumbling for

breath and gnashing clods of rubbery weevil-ridden
pigeon peas from crumpled enamel mugs and maggot-

riddled maize *nsima* on holed rusty plates, besides,
denied the luxury of cutlery in those flaming beacons

of prison visible at night from where you stand, this
bundle of memories is not your Peter knocking on his

disciples' church door nor Lazarus resurrected, this is
your Mulungusi Avenue rebel uncle returning from

that eternal abomination to which they slung him –
'Could I give your auntie the fright of a lifetime call?'

The Risen Lazarus at Very Tedious Last!

I used to wonder about the details of the risen Lazarus
Not merely how thankful he must have been to Jesus for
Raising him from the dungeon of death after four days
Nor the unbelieving bystanders, startled then stupefied
But how Lazarus managed to get up with hands and feet
So tightly strapped by ribbons of death, his face blinkered
Like a hostage; how he must have bashfully wriggled as
They sheared the shroud after Jesus had intoned, 'Untie him'
I dreaded his rotting body too, once catacombed always
Even Sister Mary conceded, 'Lord, four days, the stench!'
And does the tomb stench just disappear at resurrection?
What welcome tears ran down their cheeks, what embrace?
And were Martha's hot porridge and Mary's warm bath
Water sprinkled with crushed herbal roots and leaves to
Sever Lazarus from the dead as we do when the prisoner
Is released from Mikuyu, say, after three and half years?

What bothered me above all and I fear bothered Lazarus
As well was the global truth that there would be no second
Time, once Lazarus died again, after Jesus Christ had really
Gone, there would be no second time for Lazarus to return
To his beloved sisters until perhaps the very final day. So
Now that this Lazarus is home and dry, the stars inmates
Scrambled over in the Mikuyu Prison cells are for grabs,
This Lazarus must watch every assembly, ritual and feast
Of the Sanhedrin for those further charges the Officer-in-
Charge noted at send-off; those mates Lazarus once knew,
The company he cherished, the bottle particularly – he will
Have to ruefully bolt and though it's fear of the everlasting
Pit that baffled Lazarus, it must have calmed his nerves
To feel again that dusty clay of home at very tedious last!

The Sinful Scribe of Kabula Hill, Blantyre

I

You recognised her by the way she was
Slipped into your office by the despot's
Drivers and messengers without fanfare
You inspected the name that was meant
To be your secretary (weren't you at her
Interview and her appointment?); today
You saw another face that did not match
The qualifications you had anticipated
This was recommended by the highest
Authority, 'Came from above,' you were
Told. You dared to invent a fib, 'Which
Malawi Young Pioneer Paramilitary Base
Did you indicate you had got your driving
Licence from, as I recall your application
Forms?' Often you needed no loaded lies
But only charged her to type your memo
To the censors on *Animal Farm* banned.

II

Today after your three years and seven
Months in detention, she dashes after you
Anxious to tell her story, she swears by
Her ancestors all she knew was typing
She did not do what the other secretaries
Were famed to do, now she just wanted
To say she'd been bothered by the letters
She typed for her master, your colleague
Once, elucidating your verse to the higher
Authorities when they still kept you inside
This thing's been chewing at her heart these
Years – the poor scribe forever had a heart!
Now that you are unchained she thought
She might snatch this opportunity to recount
Her tale but she must catch her bus, 'Thank
You for your attention.' Wait, you interrupt
Blessing! Absolution! Lord, is she gone! you
Open the confessional for the next sinner.

Another Clan of Road-fated Shrews

No, they have not gone, the cockroaches that
Snuffed the radiant hue of our calabashes
And crashed on the walls of our prison cells
Where their shadows tracked us down; we
Were foolish to assume they would retreat
Into the crevices of their pallid orders those
Vipers now changing their skins shameless;
We should not have anticipated their nerves
Screeching and springing branch to branch –
Watch them darkly even! Must we therefore
Cede to another dance whistling yet old tunes
Like we have not been circumcised harshly,
Must we surrender to the sallow faces which
Consigned these brittle bones to the reeking
Pit we happily left behind? Do I dare to linger?

No Mother

Excuse this arrogant spectacle but with such
Furrows of tears on your daughter's breast
And the children's nimble cheeks, I will not
Chameleon colour another life. Why must I
Who've suffered everything, conceding none,
Inflict on your daughter, these children, more
Weeping verrucas from the cockroaches that
Have sucked their feet for slaying nobody? I
Will travel, however briefly, however painfully,
I will assemble drier twigs from distant ravines
For the fishermen's bonfire of another dawn.
I will venture far away where navels of alien
Hounds inspire mothers to conceive squirrels
And not the road-fated shrews that we are!

The Vipers Who Minute Our Twitches

'Son, venture into distant rolling terrain
And marvel at God's umbilical cordage
Of peculiar hounds', Uncle, this abrupt
Liberation, this dogged fear for our safety
From friend and foe is cause enough; may

These wavering village voices therefore,
These distressed handshakes of relatives
Who tremble to see us off, hurt; when did
Our political dissenters ever procure proper
Goodbyes from their dearest ones here?

So let the families of your kinsfolk dear,
Let these nephews and cousins mustered
In defiant solidarity make their hurried
Backhanded hugs before the informers
Gathered about register who was present

At these rebels' send-off, though what galls
Us now, if we are truly free, is whether ours
Are the last feet to abandon this beloved
Territory in disgrace for having lynched no
one; is this the ban we so dearly dreaded?

May our expatriate defender in light T-shirt
Shrewdly extend his welcome wink then,
May he walkie-talkie our delayed arrival
To his compeer upstairs, we'll feign smiles
In wonder, irritation and beholden shame!

And yet what spectacle my dear country,
What affront, what treason deserves this
Protection from you by kinder friends from
Far away? When did your warm heart go
Cold? And should we perhaps shake this

Tenacious dust off our blistered feet against
This beloved soil? What crime merits such
Covert parting on exit visas, exit air tickets?
And these children, these buoyant children
Where will they get anchor to repair and ride

The battering swells of their foreign confines?
And this resilient wife, this house of gentle
Friends, what breach have these committed?
Uncle, which airport are we bound for, what
Story shall we claim we have landed to tell,

Which navels of alien hounds are we meant
To wonder at with our stubborn brood of folks
Left behind? And how long, Lord, will the vipers
Minute every twitch, laughter and tone of voice
Made by those sending off this rebel family?

II   *Impressions of Exile*

The Delights of Moving House, Tang Hall

When we first arrived in Tang Hall
the children welcomed us by stealing
glances at us, sniggering over the hedge
milling about the front door hedge after school
spitting loudly, monkey-faking without ambiguity
until some started throwing eggs at our windows
sometimes writing 'FUCK OFF' on the windscreen
of the car we had bought near the scrapyard

Judy's laughter fired
'How dare crowds of Tang Hall kids do this to chaps
rescued from the jaws of African crocodiles?'
Lunda joked
'I wish they gave us the eggs they waste on our walls!'
Lika merely sulked as he mended his bicycle
Mercy frenetically mopped the kitchen floor
shouting, 'Hold on, children, what lies here?'
and I thumped my chest recalling my Latin
'Mea culpa, mea culpa, mea maxima culpa.'

Our friends at Newton Terrace, Bishopthorpe
Nether & Upper Poppleton, Oxford, Edinburgh
and places were nonplussed
and Amanda Webb our youthful landlady
who'd lived here throughout her degree at the university
brought her dad to placate our hostile hedge with his smile
but the Tang Hall eggs splattered on until
Father Austin O'Neill's prayer and Police Constable Bailey
interfered to scatter the throng of Tang Hall youths

When John Craven suggested Mercy's
re-training at York District Hospital
Amanda invited us to her plush wedding
and Nancy Reed across the back garden hedge
proposed that the children
share her cuppa
and afterwards always waving her greetings
over the fence
or popping over with her birthday card
and bunch of flowers for each child's birthday
she had kept in her diary

then Mercy sent Nancy my book of verse
for the squalor of the prison wagtails
to chatter with her at Christmas
(what of the electric mower she lent us
to speed up our chores, spruce up the lawn,
tidy our trim) until Mrs Amanda Tiddy's
house was full with the children's
school friends sleeping over.

Today as Mrs Tiddy's house is up for sale
and Walmgate Removals are finally here
our neighbours have begun grinning
at us tendering belated offers
confounded by their belief that we have
not yet seen the splendid beaches of Whitby
Scarborough, Bridlington or their
Yorkshire moorscapes scrolling in pink, green, brown
like dyed canvas outstretched on dunes

As we move house today and the New Year
braces for another bitter Pennine winter
some neighbours are wondering why
we could not stake a Council House
or squat with blankets and pillows
actually on the pavements of Seventh Avenue
didn't we know that was one way
the Housing Authority could tell
we were neither lying nor meaning
to jump the ageless housing queue?

And tomorrow as I run my creative rounds
across the Pennines, after my ration
of Express Regional Railways where trolleys
dampen appetites for sandwiches and coffee
tomorrow I intend to span these nipping
snow slopes of County Durham and freeze
through the red roses of Lancashire
punctuated by Chorley cakes and tea
or the shyer vernacular jokes of Frankland,
Wakefield, Garth Prisons, tomorrow I
suck in the blizzards of Leeds, cough out the charcoal
of Sheffield, shirk the drizzle of Manchester before
Liverpool's mist malingers in peeling plaster –
to nail this glory of another alien louse!

Parable of My Renault 4 Driver

It's like the story of any driver
In my part of the fourth world

There is a knock on the door
He's heard I've purchased a fifth-hand Renault 4

The guy nextdoor has just got his licence through him
He proudly displays the credential that's done the trick

The fellow must worry about anything he touches
But six months later, I get my own driving licence too

Then the real bargaining begins
Do I seriously want to see him begging at the market?

The best way to celebrate my first-attempt driving licence
Is to get him a job among my friends or colleagues

He makes no effort to conceal the intended blackmail
He believes I have enough clout

I casually suggest the police station
We part company in rather inconsonant smiles

A year later, his vehicle is policing roadblocks
Our story is sealed in mutual grins

Until recently, exactly sixteen years later
I am madly trying to send a message to England

From the post office of his rural district
Where they exiled my wife at their hospital

(To punish her for my sins –
She now enjoys feeding the border fugitives

At weekends particularly
Sharing with the malnourished fugitive babies

Those priceless vitamins
She often brought to my prison cells)

On the phone I accentuate each point
With my now familiar chorus

'Yes, three years, seven months, sixteen days
I have been released unconditionally...'

But a booming voice behind me jolts
My British Council telephone conversation

'You are the most dangerous man I've had to deal with!'
I duck, to confirm it's not another arrest

My Renault 4 driver's tale then unfolds:
After the police, he went to the post office

Where he's had the enviable duty
Of sorting out all my protest mail

'Bags upon bags arriving from the world each day
Where on earth did you get these friends?'

He apologises to my wife,
He could not even greet her when I was still in

For fear of recrimination;
'But those bags upon bags –

Some we sent to your headmaster
Some to the Special Branch

Others to the Secretary to the President and Cabinet
A few books and magazines

We managed to derail to your wife here.'
But he mustn't talk too much,

He must be off, wishing us well.
Today, from another corner of the globe

When this Stavanger pub in Norway recounts
And Bergen Philharmonic Orchestra underscores

The extent of the war of my liberation
The parable of my Renault 4 driver still meddles.

St Margaret Clitherow of York

As the Yorkshire fox of this leafy autumn howls
your rebel spirit Mrs Margaret Clitherow
mocks the wondrous asylum my African
village wisdom warned about:
in far-out lands expect to find
hounds with weird navels,
Mrs Clitherow the breach for which
York Sheriffs and Bailiffs gaoled you in York Castle
then in Kidcote-by-Ouse-Bridge crushed
four hundred years on, your saga unnerves;

Why do tyrants forever unleash provocateurs
to ensnare harmless recusants? Why did
York Sheriffs seek to yoke your contest
for the rights of minor Catholics seized
by the Elizabethan connoisseurs of death
when they knew you would never
revoke your care for minority?

And when you watched through your window
between the Shambles and the Pavement
beside the Church of Holy Cross
when you saw the city's executioners erecting
scaffoldings to hang your mentor Thomas Percy
that 'dear of the whole people'
that true Earl of Northumberland
whom you beheld writhing to his
death – to the city's cheering street crowds
who relished the executioners' drama,
when Judge Clinch 'legally' searched
your heart for whatever he had sown
and prayed for you to be conformable
to his monarch's church after the travail
he fancied over his execution of pregnant
rebel women; when the executioners
quelled your bones *peine forte er dure*
after covering your groin with the habit
you'd embroidered for your own death;

Mrs Margaret Clitherow,
it was not just another
'traitor by the holy blunder of papal Bull'
they stilled for felony of harbouring priests
and sharing their bunker masses,
it was not a mere woman
tending offal-and-tripe in her husband's butchery
that the judges interrupted
it was more than your surreptitious
voice they smothered
it was a saint;

And how could the courts not think
that six weeks after secretly burying you
in an obscure filthy city corner
your ghostly father and cohorts would
re-inter, Gregorian chant, incense and all,
your 'Incorrupt body without any ill smell',
why did the rock that tore your skin
piercing your heart
that eight hundred bulk which
splintered your tender ribs
on York's Toll-Booth-by-Ouse-Bridge
why did they all conspire without seeing
that the vestige of your hand at the Bar Convent
and the lock of hair elsewhere
would forever jeer their act
why were they not ashamed
of the memory of the anniversary
when we would hallow your blood?

Saint Margaret Clitherow
as the bed-rock blasts the veins your
'Jesu, Jesu, Jesu, have mercy on me'
still echoes and in the other
kingdom remember to pray
for these blind mirrors of your
ecclesiastical arraignments
for whom you resurrect today
and will rise every October!

Heartaches in Norwegian, Bergen

As the dregs of our prison begin to settle at the bottom
of another calabash and the times start to focus, allow
me to over-indulge Helge: my dear fellow, this week I
laughed when I imagined you camouflaged as tourist
at the airport on entering my country with solidarity
messages from friends at Zimbabwe International Book
Fair, the Association of Nigerian Authors and others
tucked under your sleeve, refusing to declare, what cheer
your 'bulletins' brought smuggled into our grey prison
walls, what chatter inspired, we only wondered why
you did not wait for our reply, did you fear the border
characters would sniff the writer, critic and diplomat?

And today I arrived in Stavanger, that tip of the world
where your pine public houses hang from the cliffs as
thrashing waves roar below, our umbrellas perpetually
dripping, today, I drank your Skol on tap too touched
by the Norwegian sagas of your struggle for our rescue
from our despot's crocodiles; and I visited the suburbia
of Bergen as you insisted, the snow capping the knolls
dazzled blind; we even skidded for Bergen Philharmonic
Orchestra where flutes wailed for the liberation of other
souls trapped in the distant dungeons of another globe.

But that buoyant little theatre in the heart of Bergen and
Ariel Dorfman's tale it told, in Norwegian so accessible,
that was another time in another territory; for the woman
who struggled to free herself from her torturer, that wife
forced to take on a midnight lodger (the lodger whose car
had broken down on his way home and the husband had
wanted to play his Samaritan), the woman was raped by
the prison superintendent turned her midnight lodger,
she was viciously violated in the jail she was freed from;
nor is her anguish idle, for, isn't the woman the icon for
the ruthlessly raided who are forever forced to reconcile!

Watching Berthe Flying Easter Balloon

I

When Michiel decided to surprise his mother on
Her seventieth birthday at Easter, he had no idea
How it would go. 'Let's give her a treat of her
Lifetime, let's fly her in a balloon!', he offered; at
First Berthe's children and grandchildren laughed,
Then they decided to give it a shot. 'It'd be great
Fun to watch granny floating in a balloon!' giggles
Michiel's cheeky little Ivy. And Berthe lingering on
Their real intention takes them on, Ludo assuring
Her she'd not fly alone, he'd sit right next to her;
Martin & Connie then invite us to cross The Channel
And watch Berthe flying the balloon; we all accept.
But it was the greyest April day in Rhoon Village;
The cloud thick; it began to drizzle; Michiel felt
A lump. Why does Rotterdam go suddenly foggy?
Perhaps it wasn't a good idea. Shouldn't we have
Gone to church first? Then the Balloonman rings:
It might be too risky to fly, but he'd get back to us
When the fog clears. Michiel's lump is heavier; then
Ludo, Martin and the children put on their anoraks;
We all put on our anoraks; soon we are combing
The garden's rose shrubs, trees and flowers, calling
Out the Easter eggs we are each picking – the Dutch
Easter has truly begun, balloon–flying forgotten.

II

When the cloud clears Balloonman rings again, 'Let's
Give it a try'; Berthe's face beams; we run to waiting
Cars; Michiel looks lumpy, we jump in with him to
Give him a cheer; Martin & Connie trail us, rather
Shaken too. But to fly a balloon from Tilburg Park,
Gather those with families flying; together pin down
The basket bottom as the top rest gas-blows into shape;
(On soft, murky grass it won't be easy). Berthe & Ludo
Haven't got all the time to jump into the burning basket!

'Isn't it nice, other families are flying as well?' Michiel
Only grunts. The lift off is rugged at first then sways!
'Oh, watch that swamp now; Lord, those tall trees!'
And Berthe is gone; but return to cars to give chase.
Balloonwoman who communicates with Balloonman
Makes our guide (though Michiel wonders if any
Person really knows where Berthe's balloon intends
To perch); so, we mustn't take long to re-fuel the cars
(Or stop to pee); Michiel's getting sour about these
Tedious green fields, the dykes and canals Berthe
Is crossing; when the basket appears to want to land
On a colony of ugly trees, Michiel's driving stops!
We resume nervously waving to Berthe flying lower
And lower until the basket swings, swoops, jerk-lands
On Maren-Kessel farm where caged hounds bark: well
Done, welcome, welkom! Balloonman's glad he's landed
This Catholic side of River Maas; the Calvinist side
Wouldn't let him pick up his balloon Sunday last time;
Balloonman displays his Tilburg letters of credence,
Berthe receives her birthday flying certificate, Michiel
Touches Berthe's bruised hand with sparkling smile!

Chronicle of an 'Other' Imperial Child's Encounter

I

Today this little city voted the Cultural Capital of
Europe last year radiates with world bards brought
Here to celebrate another night of poetry on the road
But why don't we make the local cultural viewing
Rituals first, why don't we catch those exuberant
Brushes of Peter Paul Rubens as they shimmer in their
Lustre of antique leather on the walls with Rubens'
Self-portrait glinting through the Baroque furniture
(Wasn't it his Christ's 'Descent from the Cross' I
Saw many London student years ago?) No matter
But what chairs, what 'Rubenshuis' cabinets craftily
Chiselled with their edges perfected by Hercules whose
Sinews cuffed battle the lion beside flying archangels
'... And these concrete images of heads on these walls
Are the philosophers Rubens and the Archduke read...'

II

Yet watch, gently the city's regal esteem and images of
Another perfectly buried childhood spontaneously surface
Among the merry minstrels wired into Antwerp's cheer-
fully restored theatre, is it to mock our person or our verse
On the road? Never mind; I served Mass beside Mulanje
Cedar altars once and after ensuring that their flaming
Easter candles did not touch the winged wooden cherubs
And seraphs, I knelt down, offered my confiteor, crossed
Myself and left little expecting this encounter with other
Original altars in Antwerp; ah, how the ancient sculptors
Might have forever deftly carved their oak as Rubens
Held his luminous court brushes! Watch, Lord Macaulay's
Africa choking under her village fig trees: 'Name Europe's
Two largest harbours', confused hands up, the chorus
Throws up its mechanical 'Rotterdam and Antwerp!'

III

Then envision subtle colonial Arithmetic on London;
Foxed under mission fig trees those pristine villages
Ago, we marvelled as imperial choo-choo trains left
London Euston Station at six for Liverpool Lime Street
Two hundred miles away; if the trains travelled fifty miles
An hour, what time would they arrive, all being equal?
Our answers splash down David Livingstone's cataracts,
Surfing past the baobab trees of our Kasisi Traditional
Authority, nibs spill out ink as bounteously as bee-eater
Droppings adorn our Bishop Mackenzie's grave stone!
Or take only the other month, when Wakefield prison
Nursery rhymes our prime encounter 'Here we go round
The Mulberry Bush, Mulberry Bush, Mulberry Bush...'
How jealously the prison officers guard this primeval
Bush of Yorkshire for other buried imperial children –
It's remarkable how our vulgar imperial idols mellow
With time, sometimes towering, to tone us down!

On His Vain Search for Roosendaal

In vain did your firefly cross The Channel, hoping
To avoid the stinging fog of the vale of York, landing
Among the ancient windmills and the mute mazes
Of the dykes the Dutch forever reclaim from the sea;
In vain did your African firefly burrow among these
Vandyke brown leaves of autumn choking the criss-
cross of canals, cluttering the serpentine dykes; in vain
Did your firefly drift with the swans and ducks or float
On these purple-blue knots of waterlilies, bemused by
The leaping fat frogs of Leiden; in vain did the firefly
Watch the dexterous Dutch invent tropical weather and
Tropical gardens where they grow the delicious cherry
Tomatoes you loved to swallow whole once; in vain
Did your firefly comb these restaurants where sizzling
Biefstuk Mozart vies with *Tong Picasso*; in vain your
Epic quest for his Roosendaal that netherscape virginal
Valley of roses where weed and serpent slumber among
The radiant roses as firefly gurgles from the bitter herbal
Concoctions of the gourds of underworld hunchbacks
Who hold the key for opening the doors to our follies;
In vain did firefly hack through thorny plots of Dutch
Women shouting their tulip prices and brightly clad lads
Their Edam cheeses; in vain all that; for today firefly's
Feeble feet began to tire over Roosendaal's antiques of
Those squiggles of signature scratched on Den Haag's
Groeten uit Holland postcard he received in prison far
Away which he came to these netherscapes to recover;
And last night the snow was heavy; the vista around 272
Boerhaaverlaan is as white as coconut fruit split open,
The pigeons are gathering outside the window, scraping,
Pecking at the heaps of snow and cooing as if to mock
Your firefly's wasted hunt for his Roosendaal; let your
Yorkshire dales spring then, however scornful the harsh
Echoes of home, fix it for this firefly to scrape the snow-
laden hedges of Yorkshire; as for his Roosendaal, there
Will be another autumn to hunt the Dutch briars!

Another Guide to Clifford's Tower, York

When Border TV crew suggests that I try to annul
Some horrors of Clifford's Tower through Africa's
Peculiar prison lenses, the Tower's guide protests:
How daft! but I refuse to condemn lest the cracker
Has recycled so many terrors for other callers that
Our Border TV cameras perhaps scare his received
Creed about Clifford's Tower. And indeed today
Eight hundred years on the city still tends Clifford's
Tower in golden daffodils which bloom throughout
The Yorkshire spring and when Guy Fawkes comes
Round each year, you must gather beside the Tower
In balaclavas and winter coats to worship the local
Hero, watching your children watching fireworks
Fabricating rainbows in the dark sky but as you rub
Your tingling hands against Yorkshire's freezing
Breeze, do not weep with the willows of River Ouse,
Let the willows' dreadlocks hang loose like the sausage
Tree fruit you left by the River Shire many mountain
Ranges away; consider, rather, these to be the navels
Of those eccentric hounds of exile that your fathers
Warned about, your reward is the cool beer beside
The warm gas fire later; and remember to shout with
The children as their flaming Guy Fawkes shatters;
And forget Roger Clifford the Lancastrian rebel they
Harshly hanged after the Battle of Boroughbridge
Naming the Tower after him; forget the Sheriffs and
Bailiffs who summoned one hundred and fifty Jews
To burn themselves to death at the Tower for spurning
Insolvent authority and refusing to quash their loans
After the English King and defender of Jews had gone
On Sabbatical in Burgundy; and if the story of those
Jews who first fomented the daffodils in thoughtful
Memory of their own dead moves you, riddle out
The wilful tone of your guide to Clifford's Tower!

The Acacias of Gaborone City, Botswana

When I first saw these acacias of Gaborone
I flinched at their stubborn roots once harshly
shattered by the cruel bombs of apartheid,

I wondered why their leaves insolently opened
up when their brute branches and keen thorns
tore our careless hands as the brown sparrows

Teasingly hopped about the creamy flowers;
I feared how their grey blended with our hazy
landscapes too and wished their jacarandas were

Likewise fabricated to shield our barrenscapes;
but today when I watched this capital branching
in all directions and like other world capital cities

Quietly breeding dual carriageways, I sighed
at their latent malignancies as the chirruping
sparrows succumbed to the countless car alarms

Tweeting from house to hut; even you thought
of planting more acacia trees around your house –
to scratch some thief to shame! you despaired.

Warm Thoughts for Ken Saro-Wiwa

I was beginning to recover from the gruesome
Gecko which burst on the blanket rags on my
Knees after severing from the cobweb rafters
Of my Mikuyu Prison recess when I heard that

The armed vultures had abducted you again,
My heart aches. I remember your gentle embrace
At Potsdam to salute my release from another
Choking cell, you recalled the freezing breath

That writers globally sprayed on our lion's balls
To loosen its flesh-clutching jaws, I bragged about
The fleas and swarms of bats pouring stinking shit
Into our mouths as we battled the eternal beasts

Of our wakeful slumbers; you laughed. Today,
You must invoke that humour again, my brother
And as you marvel at the handcuff scars darkly
Glistening, courage. Watch the cracks on your

Prison walls, let them nimbly hold the razors and
Needles of the life we once endured, let the rapture
Of gracious laughter shared, the memory of justice,
Succour you like a prayer then as those countless

Scorpions, mosquitoes and cockroaches fuss about
Your walls, remember to reach out for that tender
Cloud which forever hovers above your solitary
Sanctum with our wishes to restore, cheer, hope!

Reply to Ken Saro-Wiwa's Letter

Dear friend
your reply to my verse arrived
too late
too late to save you
too late to save our hope for your smile
severed
by the general's executioners.
So, now that
General Abacha Shells and his henchpeople
have executed our Ken Saro-Wiwa
they can settle down
to their prawn cocktails
mapping out new paths
to dupe the heads
of our biltong-dry Commonwealth
defying the moratorium of global appeals
mocking our efforts made on behalf of
justice.
Yet if the executioner and his henchshells
can really murder a mere Ogoni
they must sharpen their state and company
machete hacking premium disclaimers beyond
'This is War' and 'We are only there for the oil!'
Oh humanity, who does not know
commerce and politics must never mingle
under the stress of human dignity
and market forces?
So, let Abacha Shells' henchpersons
unleash their leeches to suck the blood
of the vociferous placarders they invent
tracking the rebels down smoky alleys
as they leap over the broken bottles of their lives
along narrow backyard streets of another history
synthetic rucksacks on their backs
flying from airport to airport
piece work to piece work;

Let General Abacha Shells and his henchmen
who have murdered our inventive joker
deny it;
For today as we chant your prayer
'Lord, take my spirit but the war continues',
we pledge congress with you Ken Saro-Wiwa
we will stoke the pipe with you
forever defiantly puffing
aluta continua!

NyaRwanda Among the Bones of Butare

Why have I come to watch this carnage of machete
Slashing each other's banana fronds to death in this
Eternal heat? How do I hope to find a lost friend
Among these godless shrines of Rwanda? Isabela,
Those milky teeth you showed me when you said
Farewell at our language seminar exactly eleven
Years today are stained in blood. I feel hollow and
Cheated. I sat under the canopy of your banana
Leaves as the chicks pecked at their morning grain
You promised to teach me real KiNyarwanda as
I could not join the others climbing your mountain
Ranges, and as the village children gathered, keen
To share my first lesson, laughing and bemused by
The words I used – why did they sound like theirs,
I jotted down fifty words in KiNyarwanda from my
Corpus of limited ChiYao from home two thousand
Miles away, the children thought I was lying, I spoke
Their tongue, how could we communicate so easily?

I asked about your banana beer, what did you blend
To produce the delicate flavour so congenial, how
Many days did it need to brew, did you sell it from
The tattooed melon-shaped calabashes I bargained
For at the markets we stopped over, driving between
Kigali and Butare, where you chose two souvenir
Kitenges, black on white and white on red, for my
Wife to wrap-round? Besides, that pristine Marimba
Orchestra which toured all France in summer, you
Boasted, and which we loved so much at Butare – has
All that come to this? Why did you not warn the Hutu
And Tutsi mementoes I arrogantly clutched would
Soon rend each other to death, human flesh floating
In lakes, rivers and streams like dead leaves? Where,
Where are the gentle children who giggled at my first
Syllables of KiNyaRwanda, where in this desecrated
Dust of exodus, this stench of human meat, amongst
These arid bones, NyaRwanda, where are you now?

The Child That Now Hurts

(A poem for Rwanda)

This child that hurts today was hers
once, sleeping soundly on her back,
braced by glowing *kitenge* as mother
worked the ridges of her millet field

This son that whimpers in his sleep was
the son she pined for once upon years,
when he cried mum breast-nourished
him under the shade of her succulent

Banana fronds; this boy turned bones
strapped on mum's emaciated back was
hers, running up and down the sausage
trees of her millet field, inventing cars

From contraptions of bicycle spokes and
clothes-hangers, becoming the man who
would weave the reed and bamboo granary
for her millet harvest. But when the war

Eventually came, the war between mum's
brothers' houses, this war without a name
when this alien encounter spilled bloody
heavy rains, washing away foundations

of sausage trees, millet fields, the bananas,
men, women, children, goats and chickens;
when the grass-thatched houses began to
crumble, swirling, floating away, mother

Had to run for her life, the son on her back
unable to reap the millet of her sweat; now
having crossed the thorny bushes, craggy
cliffs, steep hills and valleys in the exodus

Of this hostile amalgam of dust and blood,
this blood whose roots no mum or child
can fathom; today, when his mum's feet
refuse to lift, badly blistered in her run from

The enemy – her own people; today when
the child on her back gets too ponderous
and the strings of *kitenge* biting severely into
her shoulder's flesh snap; even the mother

Must retire and lay her son by the way-side
for the foraging hyenas to assault – better
that indignity of ravaging beasts than dying
with his bones forever girdled on her back.

The Healing Scalpels & Smiles of York

I thought I should offer you a bouquet of white roses
my favourite carton of Belgian chocolates
and a large thank-you card
for stripping Mercy's varicose veins
and nipping off the spite of her cancerous breast
I thought you might like a casket of Malawi export tea
or the pristine carvings of Mulanje prime cedar
for the pins you have conjoined my bone to bone
stretching the left tendon for a better heel
to diminish the lament of this exile club foot
but I know no postcard, no flowers
no image carved in choice wood, no chocolate, no tea
to adequately reward your delicate touch
for the gentler faculty of the limbs
you have deftly realigned

I thought you might like my brother's story instead:
as Matthew cycled down the ghostly valleys
of Kadango Village to CheNamalaka's
those tender years ago
I settled on his bicycle carrier
then the brakes snapped half way down hill
and after tough, sharp, gurgling bumps my foot slipped
tangling in the spokes that chewed it
and what torture, what blood that spouted;
if the village elders had not cast the foot in reed
and four decades later, three years, seven months
sixteen days of skipping without rope in life-despot's prison
had not ravaged the tissues and nerves,
the radiance of your genial nursing would have
caressed a different malady, another Plaster of Paris
and why did your colleague at Malindi Anglican Hospital
not choose his leave after the village elders
had cast my foot in reed paraphernalia? No matter

When I revisited my village of birth recently I
spotted the valley my brother and I plunged down
and after pausing on the gravestone where
cancer buried Mercy's dad at only 44
I thought you might like to hear another tale
to balance your healing scalpels and dislodging smiles!

Chitenje for a Lifetime Wedding Cheer

And tonight when the uncles, aunts & elders
Gather beside the nervous light of the flaming
Candles & paraffin lamps; when they spread
Their ancient mat, from timeless baobab tree
Trunks, on your floor & they invite you both
To consummate their exhortatory tales of heroic
Wedlocks of long ago; neither weep at their
Bawdy tales nor waste your lamentation in silent
Capitulation; for you are nobler people, neither
Bonded to the elders nor their tales & mind these
Elders, they tend to define things in easy black
& white; you deserve subtler shades of colour;
God has endowed you with rare brown delicately
Drenched in rare pink wedded to precious love;
So, when we offer you this traditional hoe, this
Chitenje, we do not mean you to dig the rolling
Green valleys of Wales or mystic mountain ranges
Of Malawi; for hoes are signs & *chitenjes* mere
Covers – outward icons. The serious business of
Love & tolerance begins when you smile after
Your first quarrel & eyes sparkle at each parting;
May this hoe then, this *chitenje* & these words
Bring you the wedding cheer of a lifetime, love!

III   *The Return of the Rhinoceros*

The Return of the Rhinoceros

(letters home)

I

We all feared their return would be a matter of course
Those petrifying rhinoceros of Liwonde Game Park
Now safely tamed among the elephants and hippos
Of home, it's a shame it took so many innocent snouts
And horns, so much bloodshed of brother kill brother
Take task, shame it took so many sweating armpits
So many bloody festivals, the prayers, warm thoughts
These years, to realise that sooner or later we would
Have to restore this badly jaded Liwonde Game Park,
Giving back the precious rhinoceros' snouts and horns
We foreign exchanged for swollen Swiss Accounts or
Carelessly flung to the drug arenas of Californian exiles
Where other rhinos are bravely rested – are these new
South African game rangers the Mandela syndrome
Once trusted? May their precious gestures multiply.

II

And today I remember those 'Kudya Discovery Lodge'
Hippopotami we loved so much by Liwonde Game Park
I recollect how hard they blew their noses, shooting water
Jets in the air and cheering our external examining sister
Micere fuming from our airport prudes for shamelessly
Ripping her trousers straight from Oslo instead of simply
Warning, 'Women no trousers, men short hair here!' No
Matter. So, what happened to the other hippos after your
Triumphant referendum? Did they perhaps stomp about
The reed shores of Liwonde Game Park, foaming, undone
When they saw the ancient rhinoceros returning to camp?
What tune did the whimpering Naisi pythons and Kabula
Hill cheetahs sing as you marched the jacaranda avenues
Of home? What verse crossed the Likangala and Ndirande
Bridges to cover our rebels from the wrath of the gods?

III

And should I have been there you honestly reckon
To hobble about, hit the bull's eye, perhaps help with
The Carlsberg rounds, as the rhinos returned to lodge?
In times like these your hedging vociferous chameleons
Are the least you need. But the euphoric Diaspora here
Would've loved to have been, these feverish swallows
Criss-crossing the global seasons for warmth, some even
Threatened to 'direct' your theatre in the round though
Obviously beaten by your heroic feat, they chose minor
Roles, to publicise this, expose that, as the news of those
Familiar clichés arrived – who dares claim more from
This distance? It was the spark of your initial newsletter,
The subterranean 'open' letters, the crunch of the Bishops'
Lenten Letter, mass imprisonments, riots, your indelible
Blood that did this land proud, please take our 'asante!'

IV

Yet this canoe you've scooped for us with the bitter adze
Of the pen, these rhinoceros you've brought back home
Guard with envy, nurture this rare babe in the warmth
Of the silk shawl our mothers left behind, for, haven't
We seen the return of European guards after burrowing
In the shadows of their own mirrors, haven't we heard
The sinister laughter of midnight jackals, those hyenas
Hooing, the foxes cracking eerie noises, scornful of novel
Liberated hands fumbling as they devised new charms
To outdo the magic of old cinders, who can imagine our
Old guards playing it otherwise? They too will attempt
To desperately remint new alliances and as the world
Has short memory of our funereal eyes irked by the end-
less wakes our guards have hatched, won't they chime:
'In the name of truces, don't take us to courts'? Watch.

The Tyrant's Game of Football, 1978

Now that our national football team brings
Home the coveted East and Central African
Football Challenge Cup and the announcer's
Husky excitement with the winning goal still
Blasts our wireless, reverberating between
Blantyre and Nairobi, may the dustbin tom-
toms of Ndirande township, the midnight
Buckets of Soche Mountain and the scratchy
Rhythms of tin-cans throughout the territory
Clamour with rapture unknown to applaud
The nation's singular accomplishment and
Why should the children for once not dance
To their troupe's triumph though to achieve
Is to commit a crime here, let the band crack
The country's banned casks of mirth – when
This babe let out its first cry, grannies and all
Jumped with joy, breaking its umbilical cord
But their hurrahs were deflated by the Father
Of the nation-for-life who saw such humour
As rebellion against his might; yet as the boys
Bring their cup, we'll claim the village dance
Again, prancing about dusty roads, shuffling
Along murky sidewalks festooned in khaki-
dry banana leaves, monkey and fox skin hats
Of long ago, today we'll make our own *nyau*
Dancers again, casting our stilts and hands up
Down, about, dancing the moonlight dance,
Defying these despotic times and when that
Party fetches the desired East and Central African
Trophy, these times of our political quarantine,
Spoof the beast into tapping his eminent-foot-
for-life and why not when the football game
He created in his life image to dim-wit sharper
Schemes these three decades has got him this
Resounding honour of his life time, so as our
Lads return tomorrow, ensnare life-tyrant into
Trebling his prize of the local tournament – we
Vow to keep away from his political football!

On His Life Excellency's House Arrest

Today when you talked about His Excellency's
House arrest under the colonial edifice of Mudi
Palace, I tried to remember when he never was!

You know how much I loathe prisons for anybody
Whether in their Mudi Palace ease or your new Red
Cross prisons (where, as you attest, the food is better,

Blankets fresh, the books, priests & doctors allowed,
The cracks on walls firmly sealed) – for arrest is arrest:
Dehumanising, abominable, shaming, vile, et cetera

How could Life President choose to die under such?
Today I had a dream of Du, Chip, Aaron, Dick & others
Plucked early by the crocodiles of the despot's heydays

We were racing in millet fields, beside Milimbo lagoon,
Competing over who could make the largest number
Of potato ridges in the least possible time; with the sun

Suddenly so harsh & the earth so adamant I beheld
Us resting on the ridges & munching golden mangoes
Whose juice dripped past our fingers, sticking, then as

We tongued the mango's honey like children, I saw
Baboons with jaws out fiercely charging, we repulsed
Them as eagles chicks & dancing triumphant sang:

> *Aweje ßane, tulyeje nsele**
> *Aweje ßane, tulyeje nsele*
> *Aweje ßane, tulyeje nsele*

* Let others die so we can eat the (funeral) rice.

Once Upon a Village

Once upon a village, there was a lone luminary,
Mbulaje-Jwine, named after multitudes of chicks
He daily slaughtered & chewed from his own

Kraal; when the village entrusted Mbulaje-Jwine
With their birdlime, their fish & squirrel traps &
Nets to catch the birds, fish & animals for them

& when he brought home several thriving hunts
They thought his lucent credentials would ensure
Their health for life; little did they fancy the ominous

Intent of another ruined child conceived on herbal
Roots from the wreck of a drunken hunter, battered
Mother & separated family. Mbulaje-Jwine traversed

The globe for years, the village hoping he would
Purge his veiled childhood transgression & conquer
The shock of the accidental murder of that female

Cousin who'd eaten without sanction the delectable
Rabbit's foot he'd brought from his triumphal hunt
& why couldn't cousin wait for the wonder-hunter

To carve the rabbit according to the village custom?
But oh, was it the heavy knobkerrie which broke
The rabbit's neck that cracked the cousin's head!

> *Aulaje ßane, alyeje nsele**
> *Aulaje ßane, alyeje nsele*
> *Aulaje ßane, alyeje nsele*

* Let him (them) kill another (others) so he (they) can eat (the funeral) rice.

Beginning Where We Left Off

So now that the senile lion has accidentally fallen
In the chasm of his own digging, let us thank the Lord
And resume the true fight we abandoned years ago

Let us begin by singing in the native tongues the old
Guards cut under the pretext of building our nation
Yet today after the monster has pulped his own cubs

Leaving the village tainted in sweat, tears & blood
Alarming his mates across the valleys, beyond the seas
Yet with his deadly crocodiles, puff-adders & scorpions

Now so submissive must we indeed gather the village
To pour libation on flaming ancestral rocks or should
We begin to roll up another sleeve for more insular

& baneful battles buried by the old legion who are not
Amused by our euphoria & are itching to avenge them-
selves? The grass huts Mbulaje's youth leaguers charred

Hacking their way among Che Moto villagers still stand
The dreaming potholes that will need our tender & those
Crocodiles & wicked amulets conceived, those untold

Cerebral malarias & tuberculoses they loved to cast
Down on rivalry, dressed as AIDS – what chaos, what
Sneer won't they raise for our freedom to requite?

> *M'bulaje jwine, n'lyeje sadaka**
> *M'bulaje jwine, n'lyeje sadaka*
> *M'bulaje jwine, n'lyeje sadaka*

* Kill another for you to eat the funeral rice.

Just Another Jehovah's Witness

The telephone message declared
you were rested below the mountain range
that splits my father's land from my village of birth
I gather you refused refuge
among the Swazi confreres who had
plucked you from the fangs of our life serpent
you preferred to rove with your father's spirit
among the hills you revered all your life
brave brother, rest in peace

You were just another frog of a Jehovah's Witness
sentenced to the squalid life of Fort Mlangeni
Concentration Camp and Dzeleka Prison chambers
imposed by our lion-for-life
and given three decades of fatal strokes
suffered by thousands of gentler frogs
in this vast mosquito-infested marshland
you should have known better,
your stroke began when the MCP red-shirts
impounded the sweat of the house you built
opposite Chikoko Bay charging you, 'These
Jehovah's Witnesses despise His Excellency's
Malawi Congress Party cards, badges...'
as they took home your beds, mattresses, pans...

And after your family had survived six
years of the insatiable malarias and choleras
at Fort Mlangeni and the tortures of Dzeleka
perhaps you should have lied about your
having repented on life-monster's terms,
when the chameleon held his temper to let
the whooshing danger pass he was lying
it was God's gift of patience he prayed for,
you should not have therefore bellowed
'How dare faceless youth leaguers sell
my house to that stupid Rhodesian?'

I first feared for your restive spirit when
you goaded my sister to abandon her tired
Anglican liturgy for your 'liberal' Jehovah's Witnesses,
and when you protested the tyrant's bid
for Chikoko Bay beach where our lion's
henchmob had evicted your friend Moyenda
from his newly built stone-brick house
without an iota of redress
'What a waste of fine beach
this beast is allergic to water!' you blared
loathing all manner of public decay
however high above it might have issued

Today I recall how you smuggled
this schoolboy under the bunkers of your
unctuous steamboat engines of *Ilala II*,
'Come, taste the pineapples and red bananas
of Mwaya, holiday with me into Tanganyika,'
you lured; thirty-two years this month
I still see your saucy smile as you settle
the white engineer's cap on your head
pushing about the packed decks, revelling
'I will sever and rebuild this ship within
weeks of arrival at Monkey Bay shipyard!'

When I heard about your stroke today
my eyes flooded for the tales of Fort Mlangeni and Dzeleka
you swore never to divulge howling
'The horrors this tyrant has loaded over
us I will chant among strangers far away',
but when I visited you at Siteki on the edge of Swaziland
you would not move pledging only to help me
uncover my *mchona* father
buried under the tractors of apartheid Braamfontein
claiming you had located him remarried
with lots of children stalking Soweto's
liberated streets, 'Could we talk?' you teased,

My dear brother, you ruled the traumas
that weighed down your turbulent years,
why couldn't you hold another heart beat
for us to gossip now that we too are freed?

Hyenas Playing Political Prisoners

'The hyenas are playing political prisoners
Now, wishing your exile well and regretting
They were not imprisoned by the monster,
Things would have been fine for them too!'

But brethren, who stopped you, who's it that
Said, 'To kill a baboon do not look into his
Face, lest you bear remorse', who's it that
Shouted, 'Enjoy while it lasts', and anyway,

Why did you pervert the recent opportunity;
Where were you when your toilet cleaners,
Your students, secretaries, messengers, drivers,
Market vendors, those urban and rural criers

(Who really felt the blisters from the chains,
Ropes and knobkerries of our monster-for-life,
His village and town youths and his pioneers
More than you and me those years ago!); where

Was this venom now unleashed when others
Fearlessly chanted for this new dawn, marching
Along the jacaranda avenues with new banners;
Why did you merely watch, stroking your dry

Chin or twisting your goatee, believing nothing
Would happen as nothing had happened before,
When everyone knew it was you who never let
Anything happen? Shame on you; pity no one

Will dare to take you to the detention camps as
You'd wish however cacophonous with explicit
Slur your voice may be today; yet knowing your
Frailty and the pest-riddled red-kidney beans in

Prison I wonder if you in particular would not
Have needed more than the ancestral tattoos
On your bottom to come back alive! Perhaps
You should have invented more brazen lore

For the monster-for-life who you informed
About us but I have a more modest overture:
Now that no one will harass you given those
New courts around you, today that you are

Back, carousing better than in your despotic
Times, why don't you do the honourable thing,
Why not embrace this truer liberation others
Have won for you? And in case you think exile

Is all colour TV and fun, let in another shadow
Tomorrow, you will see what shaved your
Guinea fowl bald, you'll feel the rabid hyenas
Of the political prisoners you seek to play!

Guilty of Nipping Her Pumpkin Leaves

I

The fear of dying without paying for those
Pumpkin leaves he pinched from her stall
Brings him here though she fiercely declares
Total innocence of the time and vegetables
She lent him seven years ago; she cannot recall
When the pigeon was 'taken' or the swallow
Wafted to those dissonant frosty habitats to
Gather twigs to nest its young after grudgingly
Revoking the blinding mirages of the sand
Beaches of the home to which he now returns;
Her vegetable hutch is still organic, though
Grown surer, but she attests vague memory
Of the pigeon and his story – Oh time, how
Could you be so callous as to sever memories
So precious when all he desires is to redress
The anguish of nipping her pumpkin leaves!

II

Her altercation becomes bolder: is he serious,
Could he have returned home to ridicule her
Nudity with his cameras as strange visitors
In the dead monster's regime once did, has he
Got no shame for asserting the resurrection
Of the best customer she once boasted about
Now presumed dead, no, she would have none
Of his alien stratagems nor would she license
Another of her own grins to enter his cameras,
Tourist or traveller, today the market deals
In graver business, grimaces of her children's
Tatters have fattened the albums of the likes
Of him before, they got the patches for their
Generous gestures instead, she would not offer
Any of her children as prey to another natty
Gimmick, never! 'Not today with the beast
Gone, never if he should decide to resurrect!'

III

'Woman, I hear your passion, I too withheld
The spite I felt for the beast to save my life
And my children but do you not remember
That son-in-law living on Mulungusi Avenue
Whom you buoyantly married your daughters
Every time he visited this stall? Do you not
Remember the groundnuts and spinach you
Lent this face that paid back each month-end?
Well, the turtle has come back home to pay
For the pumpkin leaves and okra he nibbled
From this faltering shack those many years ago;
Here, take your money which has tormented
Me in my prison and exile these many years!'
Even his London filming crew is unmoved by
His confession under the market's jacarandas –
It's not in the script for their tale of his return!

IV

Then rubbing her eyes to weigh the ghost she
Gibes in disbelief, 'They are all returning home
Those buffaloes who left these kraals many dry
Seasons ago, as for you my son, what kept you?
My daughters are too old for you now, why did
You not despatch your uncle or some emissary
For the bride price up front? Today, the price of
The pumpkin leaf you knew has more than trebled
It continues to climb though with the lion-for-life
Permanently settled the options in our vegetable
Calling are multiplying, the land is still desert
But whoever dreamt that the fiend would go for
The thundering rains to pour? Imagine no man,
No woman strips us naked for Party Cards at
The market gates any more!' Then grasping his
Hand she shoves his money into her camisole
And gazes right past him to the next patron!

The Fisheagles of Cape Maclear

I

Today it's the yellow bulldozers that lumber
Up and down the tortuous mountain foot-
paths, digging deep the roots of rocks and trees
Which block the way to Cape Maclear; cranes
Caterpillars, d-sevens, the lot, gobble rock and
Dirt blustering their way like tropical storms
The brutes mean to forge sturdy bridges over
Militant mountain valleys, rivers and hearts
Leaving behind thickets of dust for vehicles,
Bikes, mortals to saunter about; blades slash
New wounds, old wounds heal in the name
Of progress over-looked and this was rugged
Rebel country once and David Livingstone's
Dreams were mortified by mosquitoes here
No one dared enter these mountain ranges
But with tyrant-for-life now definitely sorted
The yellow monsters have been brought in
So when our jeep wailed in the dust driving
Here this morning and tourist Mozambicans
Bound for the beach were stranded, it's these
Beasts that rescued us. Today, we've deserted
The salty waters of Europe for the lap-lapping
Breakers of this lake, we've come back home
For the curative waters to cleanse the hurt of
These three decades of despotic desires; we've
Come back home to watch fisheagles swoop
Down and nestle on baobab tree branches as
Cape Maclear fishermen haul ashore twine
Laden with prime *kampango* and *chambo*.

II

So as the tender breeze blows the evening
Beach to your face, Uncle, pick up the pebbles
Skim them on the lake's temperate breakers
In memory of childhood games; take these
Beach children, bare, thrilled by the cameras
Of our London filming crew, three decades
Into independence this year, these children
Began their schooling without fees; the bold
Broad smiles declare their thirst for learning
And hoping to stir you with the Arithmetic
And English he has learnt today one child,
Having run home, offers his exercise books
To you to check, boasting fourteen, recently
Circumcised (his younger folk mock his age
And clash of customs but his resolve to learn
Is enormous); your eyes glazed by unbridled
Tears manifest the pending paradoxes of our
Predicament; you want to float away perhaps
To weep but gallantly choose the wet turtle
Canoe from where you decide to minister to
Your beach children; when our vehicle's stuck
In the sand (the mountain fool was tempting
The jeep along the sand!), you marshal your
Beach village to rescue, as I submit to distant
Colonies of huddled rocks white with seagull
Droppings and hear the island's fisheagles sing
Those familiar melodies of long ago. My dear
Uncle, welcome to the beach you spent half
Your life pining for, relish these rungs of drift-
wood as the slugs wash among the knotted blue
Waterlilies and the frogs dive underneath but
As you separate the beach snail shells you once
Gathered for porridge spoons, hear my iniquity:
When I rebelled against whoever in this land
I only thought you'd offer us another poem!

The Lies We Told About the Elephant

So when you turn over the new leaf of
This gentle nation, do not tell the children
Another lie, how wise elephant returned
To his kraal at his own fancy after years
Wandering in alien lands, how elephant
Found fellow elephants naked, starving,
Living in huts that leaked; how grateful
Elephant's folks were when he removed
Their barkcloths, showing them how best
To grow their food on farms; do not lie that
Elephants can be Messiahs that live forever;
For today, the children have watched how
Elephant stuffed himself with vegetable,
Animal, tobacco farms he fabricated all over
Their father's land to his tuneful wealth
Which the hyenas, the cats and others will
Jostle over after his long-anticipated repose;
The children have seen the palaces that do
Not leak elephant built himself; they can
Feel the nation's pulse elephant left cold;
Besides, as you restore the nation's heroes
And heroines to their glory, devote honest
Footnotes to the foreign ants in elephant's
Flaming ears who, fatigued by the infinite
Griefs the elephant forced on his own folks,
Scratched his deaf lobules with their lap-tops
Faxes, diplomatic bags, their voices and all
Do not dare another fib, for many invisible
Voices have invested in this victory of ours,
Many more than you will ever conceive!

The New Rebels at Zalewa Highway Bridge

A contraption of split bamboo and crumpled
Empty oil drums has whittled Zalewa Highway
Bridge to single file where all vehicles must stop
For traffic officers to check the bags for guns;

But as the check-point boss flicks through my
Wad of T-shirts, a soldier rushes in, swinging
AK47, bringing an urgent message for his boss:
'Sorry, Bwana, but that truck has bandits with

Two AK47s, one's loaded, come, rescue, quick';
The boss grins at our coach to proceed running
To the graver task to hand; I refuse to believe
What I hear as uneasy passengers loudly settle

Down to ponder the alien horrors of the times:
Four years ago, this check-point bustled with
Henchpeople who discharged their duties more
Ferociously, hunting the rebels they had largely

Invented to dazzle our lion-for-life; everybody was
Here: Army generals, police constables, dreaded
Young Pioneers, each boasting their own intelligence
As Romania-trained hit-squads combed the bushes

Ready to pounce at the slightest stir of rebellion;
Today this check-point is peopled by characters
Who go about their business with chatter; Young
Pioneers no longer constitute the checking junta,

'Some Young Pioneers crossed into Mozambique
On *Operation Bwezani* after the life beast's shock
On the political arena,' they shout, 'It began like
A joke, in Mzuzu city bar, four hundred miles up

North, when pioneers challenged soldiers to duel
And unable to subdue the soldiers, one pioneer
Ran home, brought a pistol, shot several soldiers
Dead; whereupon the whole battalion mounted

Operation Bwezani crushing all paramilitary
Pioneer bases throughout the land, confiscating
Their armoury, bringing about this delightful new
State! It's the pioneers who crossed the borders

That trickle back plundering villages, townships
And cities; it's pioneers, the new rebels, for whom
These check-points are raised, though God knows
Who later booted the liberators out of barracks!'

Behind me the dry mountain ranges, brown valleys
With green splashes of palm and baobab trees reel
Past as I recollect the potholes to my sister's house
And stroke my chin at the ironies of another time!

When the Watery Monsters Argued

When he revisited the Milimbo Lagoon of
His childhood he found it had rock-dried:
His dugout canoe, the driftwood, fish-traps,
The fishing tackle and the worms for bait,
Even the stubborn mudfish had moved on;

Only ghosts, watery beasts, surged forward
From the reed bushes of their barren lagoon,
Extending their wise handshakes and arguing,
'Man, neither cast this change of fortunes to
The winds nor reject your ancestral wisdom;

Do not waste your bitter herb on our bones,
We were mere messengers of your destiny;
Forget the past, forget whatever we inflicted
On you; people are now riding on the dreams
We denied them decades ago; now more than

Ever before this young nation should not be
Allowed to wallow in the past, the exigencies
Of building this glowing nation must precede
Everything and think positive, think future
Without retribution, without malice...' Yet

As the watery presences paddled their daft
Sinking raft to their fisheagle island invoking
Todays without their yesterdays, he wept at
The blisters of their future without its present,
He began to see what the fiends really meant:

He knew the silence their beastly transition
Offered was neither victory nor antidote for
The wounds the watery freaks had inflicted;
He knew that weathering their weeping scars
Would incite other bitter tears, he then swore:

'Brethren, golden glories are hard to police,
But do not ask us to forget the past, and how
Could poetry forget the past when Africa still
Bleeds from forgetting its past; empower others
To forget your past – my struggle continues!'

Notes to *Skipping Without Ropes*

My mother's language ChiNyanja has a saying which captures the notion of travel and exile central to this volume: '*Mujiyenda kuti mujiona agalu amichombo.*' Not even the English translation, 'Travel so that you can see the (strange) navels of the world's hounds' does justice to the delightful mockery, ambiguity, irony etc, embedded in the original saying. The idea is that visiting or travelling across unfamiliar borders, mountain ranges, valleys, seas, etc, is the most gratifying experience in life. Through travel one sees the most unusual hounds and the kind of navels that God has given to each; that is, one understands God's creation, the beauty and diversity of natural phenomena and human endeavour; one understands oneself better as the "other" mirrors the "self" in a special way during travel. Forced travel or exile also exposes the brutality humans are capable of inflicting on others... In this volume poems such as 'Another Clan...', 'The Vipers Who Minute...', 'St Margaret Clitherow...' and others attempt to explore the reality of incarceration and exile by exploiting this proverbial saying in varied ways.

12-13. **The Following Dawn the Boots:** Two earlier drafts of this poem were published by Amnesty International in Edinburgh Scotland and Northwestern University Press in *The Word Behind Bars and the Paradox of Exile*, edited by Kofi Anyidoho (1997); the version here is the definitive one; 'legendary gang of four' refers to Hastings Banda's four political opponents Dick Matenje, Aaron Gadama, Twaibu Sangala and David Chiwanga, who were clubbed to death by Banda's police in May 1983 though Malawians were told that the three popular senior ministers and the one MP had died in a car accident as they tried to run across the country's borders. Political prisoners' names were entered in 'Gate Books' on arrival in and departure from prison; those who brought the prisoners or got them released were forced to inscribe their names and signatures in the Gate Books for future reference. Sometimes the pages of Gate Books were ripped out to remove the officers' names and signatures as in the case of 'the gang of four' who were 'accidentalised' by Banda's hit squads; refer also to 'When Release Began Like...'

14-15. **Skipping Without Rope:** No work, no physical or mental exercise was allowed in Mikuyu Prison; walking around the courtyards as exercise was not encouraged; there was no library; no police magazine, not even propaganda for Hastings Banda was accepted; only the Bible was permitted reading though when I entered prison there were only three Bibles that were being shared by ninety prisoners; skipping without rope was the most harmless form of exercise tolerated.

16-17. **Our Doctor Mr Ligomeka:** The only clinical officer from Zomba General Hospital who had the courage to accept treating political prisoners at Mikuyu Prison when others did not dare for fear of being imprisoned too; Ligomeka was special because he fearlessly helped us communicate surreptitiously with the outside world; *nsima* is the staple meal of Malawi made from maize flour which is cooked into hard porridge; see also other poems e.g. 'Tamya's Shepherd's Pie'.

18-19. **Season's Greetings for Celia (BC):** As I was later to discover when we met at a reading in London, the full name of the person who sent me this card which arrived in prison against great odds was Celia Leak; she turned out to be a friend of my scholarship programme organiser in London in the eighties; both worked at the British Council at 10 Spring Gardens in London.

20-21. **Hector's Slapping of Mama's Brother:** Dedicated to the release of Hector Banda who was detained at Mikuyu Prison for slapping the Life President's companion's brother; when prisoners are released and you are left behind it hurts; you remember what conflicts you had with those who have been freed and wonder about the nature of your own reconciliation after release.

23-24. **Our Friend Police Inspector General:** The release of political prisoners that led to general amnesty largely because of international pressure from human rights activists, started in January 1991 when five political prisoners were freed from prisons throughout the country. These included Blaise Machila, a colleague in the English Department, University of Malawi, and George Ntafu, the only Malawian neurosurgeon, who were both held at Mikuyu Prison without explanation. In February about ninety political prisoners were released from Malawi prisons. These included twenty-two from Mikuyu. I was left behind on both occasions, never to be released. Refer also to 'Hector's Slapping of Mama's Brother'.

29-30: **The Vipers Who Minute Our Twitches:** On leaving Malawi for the UK from Lilongwe International Airport, 17 August 1991;

seen off by fearless relatives; embarrassed by but grateful for the protection provided to my family and I at home and at the airport by friendly expatriate security; see introductory note for 'navels of alien hounds' or 'umbilical cordage of peculiar hounds'.

32-33: The Delights of Moving House, Tang Hall: First impressions of exile in York; *mea culpa, mea culpa, mea maxima culpa* is Latin for 'I have sinned, I have sinned, I have sinned most grievously'; the draft version of this poem originally entitled 'Chronicle of Our Rhyming Exile' with contrived rhyming schemes was first read at a conference at Northwestern University and appears in *The Word Behind Bars and the Paradox of Exile*, edited by Kofi Anyidoho (Northwestern University Press, 1997); the version here is definitive.

36-37: St Margaret Clitherow of York: Dedicated to the memory of Charles Vivas who expounded to me the horrific tale of this wonderful ordinary woman; the search for stories of sufferers with whom the liberated can identify comes as a natural reaction to exiles; Mrs Margaret Clitherow is the embodiment of religious conflict where both Catholics and Protestants were murdered by barbarous fanatical tyrants throughout the history of Christianity.

38. Heartaches in Norwegian, Bergen: For Helge Ronning, University Oslo, and Norwegian Amnesty International Branches, 1994.

39-40. Watching Berthe Flying Easter Balloon: For Ludo and Berthe Pieters, Rotterdam, 1994.

43. On His Vain Search for Roosendaal: I travelled in vain to The Netherlands in 1994 in search of the person who might have sent me the postcard *Groeten uit Holland* from Den Haag which I unexpectedly received at Mikuyu; see 'Seasons Greetings for Celia.'

46. Warm Thoughts for Ken Saro-Wiwa: This letter was smuggled to Ken Saro-Wiwa who read it but his reply did not reach me until after his execution; parts of 'Reply To Ken Saro-Wiwa's Letter' are influenced by Derek Walcott's 'The Silent Woman'.

50-51. This Child That Now Hurts *(A poem for Rwanda)*: For and after Swanzie Agnew, Chichiri (Writers Group, 1971) and Edinburgh 1997.

52-53. The Healing Scalpels & Smiles of York: Dedicated to the Staff of Ward 14 of York District Hospital for their care after our operations.

54. *Chitenje* for a Lifetime Cheer: For George and Rebecca Harrison, on the occasion of their wedding at Durham Cathedral, 1996; *chitenje* is cloth that women wear around their waist; *kitenge* as in 'NyaRwanda Among the Bones of Butare' or 'This Child That Now Hurts' is a variant.

56-57. The Return of the Rhinoceros: Inspired by an exchange of letters from home on the fight against Hastings Banda's dictatorship which led to the restoration of democracy in Malawi in 1994; influenced by South African Game Rangers who brought species of rhinoceros to Liwonde Game Reserve in Malawi to replenish its stock which had dwindled; the symbolic implication for the new Malawi after Banda and the new South African after apartheid is patent.

62-63. Just Another Jehovah's Witness: A family history upon the sudden death of my brother-in-law Ibrahim Nyalenda; *mchona* refers to any person who went to work in South Africa, Zimbabwe, Zambia etc from Malawi and decided not to return home (*machona* – plural).

68-69. The Fisheagles of Cape Maclear: In October 1994, after Hastings Banda was democratically removed from power, I dared into Malawi with a film crew from Diverse Productions of London to record for the BBC's TV programme *Africa '95*. David Rubadiri and I visited Cape Maclear with the film crew. This piece essentially celebrates the return to Malawi and to his old post as Malawi's UN representative, after thirty years exile, of David Rubadiri, the first and finest Malawian poet; *kampango* and *chambo* are delicious species of salmon and talapia respectively from Lake Malawi. 'Guilty of Nipping Her Pumpkin Leaves', 'When the Watery Monsters Argued', 'The New Rebels at Zalewa Highway Bridge' and others grew from the experience of revisiting Malawi at other times.

70. The Lies We Told about the Elephant: A 30 year alternative history of Malawi under Hastings Banda's dictatorship.

71-72. The New Rebels of Zalewa Highway Bridge: The Chi-Nyanja word *Bwezani* translates as 'Return'; all the armoury kept by the Malawi Young Pioneer Paramilitary was 'returned' to the Army.

73. When the Watery Monsters Argued: For Dennis Brutus, Miccre Mugo, Keorapetse Kgositsile, Njabulo Ndebele and others who shared similar encounters.

Jack Mapanje, Malawi's best known poet and linguist, was born of Yao and Nyanja parents in Kadango Village, Mangochi District, southern Malawi. He went to Kadango Anglican School, Chikwawa Catholic Mission School and Zomba Catholic Secondary School. He has a B.A. degree and a Diploma in Education from the University of Malawi. In 1972 he joined the staff of the Department of English, University of Malawi, who sent him to the University of London Institute of Education to read for an M.Phil degree. His first book of poems *Of Chameleons and Gods* (Heinemann, Oxford, 1981/1991) was published as he was doing his Ph.D degree in Linguistics at University College London. Its publication raised immediate political controversy amongst the authorities in Malawi. He has also co-edited two popular poetry anthologies: *Oral Poetry From Africa: an anthology* (Longmans, 1983) and *Summer Fires: New Poetry of Africa* (Heinemann, Oxford, 1983).

After getting the University College London doctorate degree in linguistics in 1983 Mapanje returned to the Department of English, becoming head of department in 1984 and Chair of the Linguistics Association for ten Southern African Universities (LASU) an academic organisation which he helped to found that year. He travelled extensively as poet, Chairman of LASU and external examiner in Language, Linguistics and Literature in the Universities of Botswana, Zimbabwe and Swaziland; this did not please the authorities in Malawi. In June 1985 *Of Chameleons and Gods* was withdrawn from school, college, university and national libraries and bookshops throughout the country by a directive from Hastings Banda's Censorship Board. In 1987 he was imprisoned at the notorious Mikuyu Prison in Zomba without trial and without charge. After three years, seven months and sixteen days of incarceration Mapanje was released principally because of international protests from writers, linguists and human rights activists throughout the world. His second volume of poems *The Chattering Wagtails of Mikuyu Prison* (Heinemann, Oxford, 1993), conceived in prison, appeared in exile in York.

Jack Mapanje, one of the original members of the Malawi Writers Group, is a recipient of the Rotterdam International Poetry Award (1988) for *Of Chameleons and Gods*. He has run writers' workshops in schools, colleges, city centres, libraries as well as prisons throughout the UK. He has held fellowships at the Universities of York and Oxford and writers' residencies at the University of Leiden in The Netherlands and the Open University in Milton Keynes. For three years he taught African and Caribbean literature, Literature of Incarceration and Creative Writing in the School of English at the University of Leeds where as Research Fellow he is writing a book on an Africa-based fragment of post-colonial literary theory. Mapanje lives in York with his family.